WEDNESDAY'S CHILD

I0139754

Mark St Germain

BROADWAY PLAY PUBLISHING INC
New York
www.broadwayplaypub.com
info@broadwayplaypub.com

WEDNESDAY'S CHILD
© Copyright 2020 Mark St Germain

First edition: April 2020
I S B N: 978-0-88145-871-8

Book design: Marie Donovan
Page make-up: Adobe InDesign
Typeface: Palatino

WEDNESDAY'S CHILD was first produced by Florida Studio Theatre (Richard Hopkins, Producing Artistic Director; Rebecca Hopkins, Managing Director) in Sarasota, opening on 3 April 2019. The cast and creative contributors were:

BECCA CONNOR .... Brooke Tyler Benson
MOLLY STRUTT .... Susann Fletcher
MARTIN MERRIT .... Duke Lafoon
DR SUTTON .... Heather Michele Lawler
SUSAN MERRIT .... Rachel Moulton
WALT DIXON .... David Smilow
ALEECE VALEZ .... Alicia Taylor Tomasko

Director .... Kate Alexander
Scenic designers .... Isabel & Moriah Curley-Clay
Costume designer .... Susan Angermann
Lighting designer .... Thom Beaulieu
Sound designer/Supervisor .... Thom Korp

The playwright wishes to thank the Florida Studio Theatre for their hard work and commitment to WEDNESDAY'S CHILD, particularly Artistic Director Richard Hopkins, the play's Director, Kate Alexander, and Associate Artists Jason Cannon and Catherine Randazzo.

CHARACTERS & SETTING

BECCA CONNOR, *college student*
ALEECE VALEZ, *detective*
SUSAN MERRIT, *interior designer*
WALT DIXON, *detective*
MOLLY STRUTT, *attorney*
MARTIN MERRIT, *archeologist*
SAM SUTTON, *professor of biology*

Time: the present
Place: Westchester County, New York

NOTE ON MUSIC

For performance of copyrighted songs, arrangements
or recordings referenced in this play, permission
of the copyright owner(s) must be obtained. Other
songs, arrangements or recordings may be substituted
provided permission from the copyright owner(s) of
such songs, arrangements or recordings is obtained
or songs, arrangements or recordings in the public
domain may be substituted.

ACT ONE

Scene 1

(Somewhere past time)

(Sounds of the universe:meteor showers, asteroids, wormholes and the echoes of the sun.)

(BECCA CONNOR appears from darkness.)

BECCA: You'd think people would know more after they're dead, but you'd be wrong. Nobody even agrees on where we are or why we were alive in the first place. Meanwhile, we wander around, looking for someone with answers. You don't need to ask anyone who they are, you just know, and they know you too. The people who don't look you in the eyes are the suicides. And all around us are these tiny flickers of light; shiny specks floating like baby fireflies. There's a "here" and there's "back there". If you walk closer and concentrate, you can see pieces of your past, shards of color. If you keep walking you reach yesterday and the day before that, and that, as far back as you want to go. Most people don't like to go backwards. I do. I want to remember who killed me.

(BECCA looks in a direction where suddenly lights rise.)

Scene 2

(Police station—the present)

(Lights up on DETECTIVE VALEZ *sitting across the table from* SUSAN MERRIT. DETECTIVE DIXON *paces behind them, sipping his coffee.)*

DETECTIVE VALEZ: How long was Becca carrying your baby?

SUSAN: She was in her thirteenth week.

*(*DETECTIVE DIXON *gags, they look at him)*

DETECTIVE DIXON: This coffee was brewed by a sadist.

DETECTIVE VALEZ: Her door was open when you got there?

SUSAN: Yes. No! Not open, unlocked.

DETECTIVE VALEZ: Okay.

*(*DETECTIVE DIXON *sits, offers cup to* DETECTIVE VALEZ:)*

DETECTIVE DIXON: You want a taste?

SUSAN: I called her name two or, maybe, three times before I tried the door. It opened a little, then stopped. So I pushed; I didn't know.

DETECTIVE VALEZ: How far did you push?

SUSAN: Maybe two feet—just enough to squeeze in.

DETECTIVE VALEZ: How did you know she was dead?

SUSAN: She had to be! The back of her head…I told you all this before. I'd like to go now.

DETECTIVE DIXON: *(Pulls up chair)* I'd like to make happy hour at Houlihan's. Whether I make it in time is your call. You cooperate and we wrap this up, or give us attitude and we'll be here all night. We get overtime. You don't.

SUSAN: Wait. Am I arrested?

DETECTIVE VALEZ: No. *(To* DETECTIVE DIXON*)* Mrs Merrit is not a suspect.

DETECTIVE DIXON: She hired the girl and found her body. Everybody's a suspect except me.

SUSAN: I'm not saying anything else until my lawyer gets here.

DETECTIVE VALEZ: *(Finished)* You got it.

DETECTIVE DIXON: They'll send him in.

SUSAN: "Her"

DETECTIVE DIXON: I apologize for my masculine faux pas.

DETECTIVE VALEZ: Can I get you coffee, water?

SUSAN: You people really do this.

DETECTIVE VALEZ: Do what?

SUSAN: Play Good Cop, Bad Cop.

DETECTIVE DIXON: *(To* DETECTIVE VALEZ*)* Who's the Bad Cop?

DETECTIVE VALEZ: *(Getting up)* Let's take a break.

*(*DETECTIVE DIXON *and* DETECTIVE VALEZ *walk a few feet away, then stop. Since* SUSAN *asked for a lawyer,* DETECTIVE DIXON *speaks "only" to* DETECTIVE VALEZ.*)*

DETECTIVE DIXON: You're cutting her slack.

DETECTIVE VALEZ: She asked for her lawyer.

DETECTIVE DIXON: I'm talking to you, not her. She said the kid must have been trying to get out of her apartment.

SUSAN: You said that. I said it's possible.

DETECTIVE VALEZ: We can't question you without your attorney present.

DETECTIVE DIXON: She *(SUSAN)* used Becca Conner's phone?

DETECTIVE VALEZ: That's what she said.

DETECTIVE DIXON: Why not use her own cell?

SUSAN: Her phone was right there!

DETECTIVE VALEZ: Photos show Becca's phone on the table by the couch.

DETECTIVE DIXON: After she used it. Where'd she find it?

SUSAN: On the table by the couch!

DETECTIVE DIXON: *(To SUSAN)* We're trying to have a conversation here! *(Back to DETECTIVE VALEZ)* So Becca Connor dragged her bleeding body toward the door, all the way across the room and right past her phone? *(Indicates SUSAN)* Who's her lawyer?

SUSAN: Molly Strutt.

DETECTIVE DIXON: *(To SUSAN)* You can't catch a break.

DETECTIVE VALEZ: Walt—

DETECTIVE DIXON: *(To SUSAN)* You know those people who swear they were at Woodstock? Strutt never left.

DETECTIVE VALEZ: said they got your call from the apartment at 5:07. The police got there at 5:15 and you were gone already.

DETECTIVE DIXON: You couldn't stay eight minutes 'till they got there?

SUSAN: I was in shock. The blood was all over. Like little rivers.

DETECTIVE DIXON: You felt good enough to drive.

SUSAN: This doesn't make sense! Why would I hurt her? She was carrying my baby!

(MOLLY STRUTT enters.)

STRUTT: Detective Dixon! Valez! My heart sings.

DETECTIVE DIXON: *(To* DETECTIVE VALEZ*)* You hear that? She has a heart.

*(*STRUTT *shakes* SUSAN'S *hand)*

STRUTT: Molly Strutt.

DETECTIVE DIXON: *(Shows photo to* STRUTT*)* And here's Becca Connor. At least the back of her head.

STRUTT: Put it in park, Detective. (DETECTIVE DIXON *pulls out her chair)* Thank you.

DETECTIVE VALEZ: *(To* STRUTT*)* Can we ask your client if Becca Connor expected her visit?

*(*STRUTT *looks to* SUSAN.*)*

SUSAN: She would have expected either my husband or myself. We came by every night to check on her.

DETECTIVE DIXON: Where was your husband?

SUSAN: At work, probably.

DETECTIVE DIXON: "Probably"?

SUSAN: He could have taken a break. Took a walk. Bought a pretzel in front of the museum.

STRUTT: Has she been Mirandized?

DETECTIVE VALEZ: She's not being charged with anything. *(To* SUSAN*)* When you got home, what did you do?

SUSAN: I can't remember.

DETECTIVE DIXON: Take a shower, wash your clothes?

SUSAN: No!

DETECTIVE DIXON: There's always that one, pesky drop of blood…

STRUTT: We're done here.

DETECTIVE DIXON: *(To* SUSAN*)* You said you were "in shock" when you found her, but I haven't seen any shock. Just you, cheesed off we're asking questions.

STRUTT: We'd like the room to ourselves, now.

DETECTIVE DIXON: *(To* SUSAN*)* How about you start thinking about this murder.

SUSAN: Which murder? Becca's or my baby's?

Scene 3

(Before the murder—playground)

*(*MARTIN MERRIT *sits on a small horse on a spring and checks his watch)*

MARTIN: My Mother used to say that for every minute we're late we burn in hell.

*(*SUSAN *enters the scene.)*

MARTIN: Your Mother was not a happy woman.

SUSAN: *(Lights up on the playground of a fast food chain)*

MARTIN: But she was punctual. *(Looks to fast food restaurant)* You think she works at this McWhopper?

SUSAN: I talked with her once, on the phone. Work history wasn't my priority.

MARTIN: I'm wary of anybody who flips burgers that don't decay.

SUSAN: You are such a snob.

MARTIN: Which is a good thing to be right now.

SUSAN: We asked to meet her. Give her a chance.

MARTIN: *(Checks watch)* Sixteen minutes in hell.

SUSAN: Okay. Let's go home.

MARTIN: What?

SUSAN: You want to go home, let's go. We can talk about adoption, instead.

MARTIN: No, no, no. Not again. I'm not going to raise someone else's kid. You know that.

SUSAN: So many children need good homes.

MARTIN: And I hope they find one. Just not mine. *(Silence)* If we do it this way it's our child. We're the ones making our baby.

SUSAN: But she's the one carrying it. Because I can't.

MARTIN: That's not your fault.

SUSAN: It's my body's.

MARTIN: I love your body. You've got the perfect body.

SUSAN: Stop it.

MARTIN: Your mouth, your smile, your incredibly taut midriff—

SUSAN: Keep talking.

MARTIN: I could live in your belly button. And then there's that private, little mole right over your—

SUSAN: Okay! *(Pause)* There is nothing you would change about me?

MARTIN: One thing.

SUSAN: What?

MARTIN: Lose the guilt.

SUSAN: So, we're back to your Mother. *(He smiles at her. She takes his arm or hand)* There's another choice.

MARTIN: What's that?

SUSAN: We go on being happy without a baby. Put it off a little.

MARTIN: I thought you want a baby!

SUSAN: I do. But only when both of us are totally ready.

MARTIN: I'm ready. Are you ready?

SUSAN: I'm ready!

MARTIN: And this is the first time we're financially ready.

SUSAN: It's not about money!

MARTIN: That's part of it!

SUSAN: Are we planning on a new kid with every raise?

MARTIN: Is it time or not?

SUSAN: It's time!

MARTIN: You want to wait 'till we need to stick post its on our foreheads to remember to take him to pre—

school?

SUSAN: No more waiting! A baby isn't something you fit in your Day Planner!

MARTIN: Exactly! I didn't plan on you- and look how we worked out.

SUSAN: You think?

MARTIN: I know. I'm the happiest married guy who never thought he'd get married. And soon I'm going to be the happiest father who never thought he'd have kids.

SUSAN: I used to hear people say things like, "He's the love of my life" and think, "how sappy can you get".

MARTIN: And now?

SUSAN: I found my sap.

MARTIN: I found mine, too.

SUSAN: Kiss me.

MARTIN: *(He does.)* I love you.

SUSAN: You better.

MARTIN: You bet.

SUSAN: *(Spots* BECCA*)* This might be her.

*(*BECCA CONNOR *rushes in, out of breath. She wears a backpack)*

BECCA: Sorry! I am so, so sorry!

SUSAN: It's okay.

MARTIN: Take a breath…one more…good.

BECCA: *(Exhales)* I'm Becca.

SUSAN: Hi, Becca. I'm Susan.

MARTIN: Martin.

BECCA: I'm never, ever late. My Father would pull out Shakespeare on me, "Better three hours too soon than a minute late."

SUSAN: Marilyn Monroe said, "I've been on a calendar, but I've never been on time."

*(*BECCA *and* SUSAN *laugh.)*

MARTIN: My Mother said that for every minute we're late we burn in hell.

(Laughter stops.)

BECCA: That is so sad.

SUSAN: What year are you, Becca?

BECCA: I'm a Junior.

MARTIN: Do you have a major?

BECCA: It was biology but I'm switching. I can't decide between an M B A or Musical Theater.

MARTIN: Tough decision there.

BECCA: What do you guys do?

SUSAN: I guess you could say I'm a Window Dresser.

MARTIN: No, you can't. She's a Stager. She designs "Living Environments" to make overpriced furniture sell like crazy.

BECCA: Like 3-D commercials.

SUSAN: Exactly.

BECCA: *(To* MARTIN*)* How about you?

MARTIN: I'm an Archeologist.

BECCA: Awesome. When I was a kid I wanted to be Lara Croft, Tomb Raider.

MARTIN: *(Introduces himself)* Lara Croft, Indiana Jones.

BECCA: Temple of Doom?

MARTIN: You've been there.

(They shake)

SUSAN: This is not good.

BECCA: You go on digs?

MARTIN: Sure, but no dinosaurs.

BECCA: Of course not. Then you'd be a Paleontologist.

MARTIN: *(She's smart)* Exactly. I'm an Archaeological Surveyor. I excavate ancient building sites.

BECCA: *(Impressed)* Look at you.

SUSAN: Can we jump a few centuries and get back to babies?

BECCA: Sure.

MARTIN: Sorry.

SUSAN: Question: why put your body through the torture of childbirth when the baby's not yours?

MARTIN: Don't sugar coat it, Susan.

BECCA: No, it's all good. We should talk about the whole process. We need to be on the same page if we decide to go forward.

(They sit down on the plastic animals.)

BECCA: I've got questions, too.

MARTIN: You've read the Agency Contract?

BECCA: Uh-huh.

SUSAN: Does it seem fair?

BECCA: It's in the ballpark. But I'm still negotiating.

SUSAN: I didn't know you could negotiate.

BECCA: Everything but the final numbers. I want to shift some of the fees into other categories.

MARTIN: For instance?

BECCA: If I don't need Post Psychological Counseling I want it added to Compensation for missed salary. There are travel and hotel fees that won't be used since we're all here, so I want to add those to my Monthly Allowance. Do you want my breast milk?

(This catches MARTIN *and* SUSAN *off guard.)*

MARTIN: Do we..

SUSAN: We're not sure yet.

BECCA: No problem. My compensation, including insurance, is thirty-eight thousand dollars. That's with no complications, plus two hundred and fifty a week if you add breast milk. Have you hired a lawyer to review your contract?

MARTIN: We're about to.

BECCA: Can I make a suggestion? Get somebody with experience in this. It saves you money. You'll be paying, what, around seventy-five thousand dollars total?

MARTIN: Close.

BECCA: Filing anything in this County is more expensive than any other one around us. Go to any other one around us and you'll save fifteen hundred dollars. *(Takes out pack of Twizzlers)* Twizzler?

SUSAN: No thanks.

MARTIN: Why not? *(Takes one)*

SUSAN: You know your stuff.

BECCA: Your turn. Ask me anything.

SUSAN: Why put your body through the torture of childbirth when the baby's not yours?

(MARTIN sighs.)

BECCA: With business school, I'd need a Masters. With Musical Theater, I'd need an M F A for a teaching fallback. And since I don't want to sell drugs I'm selling my body instead. *(Silence)* I'm kidding. Some things are so serious it's easier to joke about them.

SUSAN: What do you mean?

BECCA: Doing this. I mean, really doing this. Creating a life. You kind of take babies for granted, but if you sit and think about it, they're these mini-miracles. Millions of people had them, but if it's

MARTIN: Do you have a baby?

BECCA: Oh, God, no. I just got out of a super-intense relationship, I can't imagine even dating again.

SUSAN: Sorry to hear it.

BECCA: Don't be. Sam was totally my fault. I got caught in a cliché. Student falls in lust with Professor and doesn't even get a better grade out of it. Right now, finding out what to do with my life is important. Being a Mother isn't.

(BECCA sees SUSAN's reaction:)

BECCA: I'm sorry. That's not what I meant. And I'm sure you wish you didn't need a surrogate at all.

SUSAN: You're right.

MARTIN: Any health problems?

BECCA: None.

MARTIN: Never?

BECCA: Appendectomy at fourteen. Broken leg from skiing. I'm violently allergic to cats. Or maybe I just hate them. I swear they hate us. If they could buy their own cat food they'd never miss us.

SUSAN: You just earned points.

BECCA: *(Puts her hand up)* Dog Person.

SUSAN: *(Hand up)* Dog Person.

MARTIN: Allergies.

BECCA: *(To MARTIN)* You'll get a copy of my medical examination. It's really comprehensive.

MARTIN: No matter what degree you get it's going to cost.

BECCA: Right.

MARTIN: Then your "fee" will only cover, what, maybe, your first year?

BECCA: But I can stay in school and have time to study. And second time Surrogates get a lot more.

SUSAN: You'd do this again?

BECCA: Who knows? I'm not even sure I'll do it now. This interview's for both of us, right?

MARTIN: Sure. How do you feel about giving up your baby?

BECCA: Whoa. It's not my baby, it's your baby.

SUSAN: I'm so glad you said that.

BECCA: All that I care about is that this baby is going to good people. Can I ask…why do you want one?

MARTIN: There are lots of reasons.

SUSAN: Martin's Father died a year ago.

MARTIN: A year next month.

BECCA: So it's a "save the family name" thing?

MARTIN: No. But when both your parents are gone it makes you see where you are in your own life. All of a sudden, you're the grown up. And every creature has an urge to reproduce. We breed or die.

SUSAN: That's Martin's version of "Baby Fever".

BECCA: I read there's really no such thing. Biologically. Otherwise, we'd all be screwing like bunnies.

MARTIN: *(Uncomfortable pause)* Interesting thought.

SUSAN: Do you think you'll want a baby of your own at some point?

BECCA: I don't know. The world's really scary now. Maybe someday if I feel like a grownup who can handle it.

MARTIN: Don't bet on that.

SUSAN: We've got so much to take in here. Why don't we all think about this and then get together again?

BECCA: Totally. Could I have your list of references?

MARTIN: *(Taking it out)* I completely forgot.

BECCA: They gave you mine?

SUSAN: They did. We'll talk soon.

BECCA: You have my numbers. I'm gonna scoot in for something greasy. You guys want a burger or shake? They have Disco Fries.

MARTIN/SUSAN: I'll pass./No, no.

BECCA: Okay! Later.

(BECCA *exits.* SUSAN *looks to* MARTIN)

SUSAN: "Everybody would be screwing like bunnies?"

MARTIN: I like her.

Scene 4

(Two interrogation rooms—the present, Interrogation Room A:)

(Lights up on DET. DETECTIVE DIXON.)

DETECTIVE DIXON: When did you hire Becca?

(MARTIN enters the scene)

MARTIN: A little over six months ago.

DETECTIVE DIXON: Stop with the knee bouncing, you're shaking my desk. Did you know Becca before that?

MARTIN: No. We went through an agency.

The knee.

MARTIN: Right. I'm just, you know, shaken up.

DETECTIVE DIXON: Now I am, too. How would you describe your relationship?

MARTIN: With Becca? She was our surrogate.

DETECTIVE DIXON: Good-looking girl.

MARTIN: She is. Was.

DETECTIVE DIXON: Very good looking.

MARTIN: And I'm "very" married.

DETECTIVE DIXON: I don't know much about this whole surrogate thing. Slow class version: You and your wife mix the batter, then the surrogate bakes the cake?

MARTIN: Don't say that to Susan. She hates 'bun in the oven' expressions.

DETECTIVE DIXON: I said "cake".

MARTIN: Either way, it's offensive

DETECTIVE DIXON: My wrist is slapped. Where were you today when we called you?

MARTIN: The Museum.

DETECTIVE DIXON: You were there all day?

MARTIN: Yes. Well, except for lunch. I wanted to get out, I walked around.

DETECTIVE DIXON: Get a pretzel?

MARTIN: *(Puzzled)* No. Just a walk. And I don't think any of the thousand people on the street would remember me.

DETECTIVE DIXON: Right. So why can't your wife have her own baby?

MARTIN: Are you serious? That is really not your business.

DETECTIVE DIXON: The girl's dead. I'm the Bad Cop. It's my business.

(Interrogation Room B—continued)

(Lights up on SUSAN, with STRUTT)

STRUTT: You can tell me anything, it's protected. I survive criminal law by pretending all my clients are innocent. You don't have to burst my bubble unless you want to plead guilty. In that case, I'm not defending you, I'm negotiating for you. Do you understand the difference?

SUSAN: Why would I kill someone carrying my baby?

STRUTT: It's where they start. *(Takes out police report)* They say your fingerprints were all over the apartment.

SUSAN: They should be. I was there almost every day.

STRUTT: You knew her neighbors, the building staff?

SUSAN: I've probably seen them all.

STRUTT: You say her door was unlocked. Was it ever unlocked before today?

SUSAN: Never.

STRUTT: So, she would have had to let someone in.

SUSAN: Yes.

STRUTT: Unless they had a key. Who does?

SUSAN: Well, I do. And my Husband. I don't know about anybody else. She gave me a set, for emergencies.

STRUTT: How far along was she?

SUSAN: Fifteen weeks. Are they going to keep me here?

STRUTT: They can't. They have nothing on you. Did your Doctors or anyone else see friction between you?

SUSAN: There was none to see. *(Deep breath)* I have to get out, now. I'm going to have nightmares about being locked up.

STRUTT: So, there's your mantra. No jail. You know how many times I've been arrested? *(Clicking them off)* Unlawful assembly, resisting arrest, defacing public property, and public nudity. That was my first time. I've protested three wars, marched for Civil Rights, Women's Rights, and Vegan Rights. And Stonewall.

SUSAN: Like Stonehenge?

STRUTT: Christ, I'm so old.

(Interrogation Room A:)

(Lights up on DET. DETECTIVE DIXON and MARTIN, DETECTIVE DIXON walking back to the table, reading a report)

DETECTIVE DIXON: Well, dog my cats.

MARTIN: What the hell does that mean? Will you tell me what's going on?

DETECTIVE DIXON: I'm surprised. That doesn't happen much. I've been here since turtlenecks. You know what a cervix is?

MARTIN: Yes.

DETECTIVE DIXON: Of course you do. You're an educated man.

MARTIN: Let's stop here. You're being patronizing.

DETECTIVE DIXON: You don't want to hear about Becca's cervix?

MARTIN: Tell me about her cervix.

DETECTIVE DIXON: It wasn't healed. Not even close.

MARTIN: Meaning…?

DETECTIVE DIXON: She had no time to heal after the procedure.

MARTIN: What "procedure"?

DETECTIVE DIXON: Becca had—

STRUTT: —an abortion.

MARTIN: *(Stunned)* She…an abortion? Does Susan Know?

(Lights up, simultaneously, on SUSAN *hearing the same from Molly)*

SUSAN: That's impossible. Totally impossible.

MARTIN: It's crazy. An abortion makes no sense.

SUSAN: How could she do that?

MARTIN: I feel kind of sick…

SUSAN: WHY would she do that?

MARTIN: Something is very wrong. Completely wrong.

SUSAN: She killed my baby!

Scene 5

(Somewhere past time)

(Lights up on BECCA*)*

BECCA: Everybody has an opinion about abortion. Opinions that never change, unless you or your Daughter need one. A woman should have control over her own body. Got it. A woman should have no control over her baby's body. Okay. Life starts at conception. Life starts when the baby can exist independently of you. And then there's sin, which would mean whoever murdered me murdered a baby killer. So, does that mean I deserved it?

Scene 6

(Police station—the present)

(Lights up in the police station. DETECTIVE DIXON's *on his phone and writing)*

DETECTIVE DIXON: What is that? Say it again. *(Writes it down)* "M…E…L" …Got it… I'm on the way.

(DET. DETECTIVE DIXON *tries to hang up his cell phone, punching the screen unsuccessfully.* DETECTIVE VALEZ *enters, angry)*

DETECTIVE DIXON: Valez, you're a millennium. How do I put this on the vibrate thing.

*(DETECTIVE VALEZ *takes the phone and drops it in the trash)*

DETECTIVE VALEZ: You are the world's biggest asshole.

DETECTIVE DIXON: The "biggest?" Are you body shaming me?

DETECTIVE VALEZ: Why did you tell the Lieutenant to take me off the Merrit case?

DETECTIVE DIXON: How many hours did you work last week?

DETECTIVE VALEZ: You think I'm making you look bad?

DETECTIVE DIXON: I think you're burning yourself out on a case that with your personal situation is not a good match.

DETECTIVE VALEZ: My "personal situation"?

DETECTIVE DIXON: How long have you and the Fire Guy been trying to adopt?

DETECTIVE VALEZ: Paul. And too long. Over a year. And you've never once,' till this minute, said a thing about it. "Great idea! Valez! You'd be a great Mother!" Or "That poor kid! Don't do that to him." Nothing.

DETECTIVE DIXON: I keep this nose out of people's business.

DETECTIVE VALEZ: Starting when?

DETECTIVE DIXON: All I'm saying is that we're on a case where somebody aborted a baby you and Fireguy would have jumped to adopt.

DETECTIVE VALEZ: How do you know? You don't have kids. Or a wife.

DETECTIVE DIXON: I have a boat.

DETECTIVE VALEZ: Do I hope we get picked to adopt a baby its mother can't raise? Absolutely. But having that baby or not having it isn't my choice. I don't have the right to make it for any woman and neither do you.

DETECTIVE DIXON: God forbid men have rights.

DETECTIVE VALEZ: They make the laws instead. And stop calling Paul "Fireguy". There's an opinion you never hide.

DETECTIVE DIXON: What?

DETECTIVE VALEZ: That I married down.

DETECTIVE DIXON: (Shrugs) Well...

DETECTIVE VALEZ: Goddamn.

DETECTIVE DIXON: Who started the war? Not me.

DETECTIVE VALEZ: What "war"?

DETECTIVE DIXON: Cop/Fireman. "Cops are guys too fat to be firemen." "What've cops and firefighters got in common? They both want to be firemen."

DETECTIVE VALEZ: Funny, I remember somebody saying, "Firefighters are guys who can't pass the police exam"

DETECTIVE DIXON: That was a joke.

DETECTIVE VALEZ: Like our wedding present? Smoke Alarms?

DETECTIVE DIXON: You've got no sense of humor. I don't like the guy because he doesn't like me.

DETECTIVE VALEZ: That's not his fault.

DETECTIVE DIXON: Whose fault is it?

DETECTIVE VALEZ: Mine. I tell him what it's like to work with you.

DETECTIVE DIXON: But you stick with me. Because I'm eye candy.

(DETECTIVE VALEZ *laughs. The tension's over)*

DETECTIVE VALEZ: The Lieutenant said staying on this case is my choice. And I finish what I start.

DETECTIVE DIXON: Do you what you want. But no bitching.

DETECTIVE VALEZ: "Bitching"? Really? Do you want me to put in a complaint? You said the same thing about my period.

DETECTIVE DIXON: Were you bitching?

DETECTIVE VALEZ: Yeah. And how many times have you bitched about your prostate?

DETECTIVE DIXON: I was philosophizing. The blood spatter report in?

DETECTIVE VALEZ: Not yet.

DETECTIVE DIXON: The scene doesn't add up. Why would the kid crawl past the phone toward her door, instead?

DETECTIVE VALEZ: She was concussed, losing blood. She wasn't thinking straight.

DETECTIVE DIXON: Or we're not. Okay, grab your coat, we're out of here.

DETECTIVE VALEZ: Why?

DETECTIVE DIXON: Forensics called. We're going rock hunting. *(Stops)* Did you ever find out who this is?

DETECTIVE VALEZ: Who?

DETECTIVE DIXON: This lady, this picture Becca taped to her fridge.

DETECTIVE VALEZ: She's called "The Madonna of the Galilee". It's part of a mosaic.

DETECTIVE DIXON: Huh.

DETECTIVE VALEZ: Those are all tiny tiles. They compare her to the Mona Lisa because of her smile.

DETECTIVE DIXON: She's laughing at us.

DETECTIVE VALEZ: No she isn't.

DETECTIVE DIXON: Oh, yes she is. Believe me. I've seen that look.

(lights down on DETECTIVE VALEZ *and* DETECTIVE DIXON, *up on* BECCA's *apartment. Sound of knocking)*

Scene 7

(BECCA's apartment—*before the murder*)

(BECCA *opens the door for* SUSAN, *carrying a bag of groceries*)

SUSAN: Hey.

BECCA: You are so amazing.

SUSAN: I really am.

BECCA: I never needed a car before, I was always on campus. What's all this?

(SUSAN *puts bags down on the coffee table and starts removing items, starting with lettuce and kale*)

SUSAN: I'm shopping for two. Green vegetables lessen the chance of a miscarriage and genetic problems. *(Another)* Olive oil decreases inflammatory possibilities in the early embryo. *(Wrapped paper)* Wild salmon. Increases blood flow to your reproductive organs.

(BECCA *takes something out of the next bag*)

BECCA: A home pregnancy test?

SUSAN: You missed your last period, right?

BECCA: Only a week ago.

SUSAN: This is for early detection, from less than a week on.

BECCA: Still… *(She looks at the box)* Can I ask you something?

SUSAN: Sure.

BECCA: Who wants the baby more? You or Martin?

(SUSAN *stops unpacking things.*)

SUSAN: We both do.

BECCA: But who wants it more? I know Martin's Father died and all, so does he?

SUSAN: I'm not sure what you're asking.

BECCA: I read this book, *The Bridge of San Luis Rey*. It's about a bunch of people who die crossing a bridge that collapses.

SUSAN: Thornton Wilder.

BECCA: Showoff.

SUSAN: Yeah.

BECCA: Something he wrote in there freaked me out. "Even in the most perfect love, one person loves less than the other." So it's the same with a baby, right? One of you loves having it more than the other.

SUSAN: And one loves less? I don't think so.

BECCA: Why not? I'm still freaked about it. When I get into any relationship, the first thing I think is— Who loves more? You must have thought about it with Martin.

SUSAN: I honestly don't think I have.

BECCA: Come on. Sometimes?

SUSAN: All right. "Love" isn't the same thing as "infatuation". When you first meet someone and you're on fire, everything's easy, it's this incredible rush. A big adventure, not a job.

BECCA: Love is a job?

SUSAN: Eventually, sure. It's work. You can say "someone loves less'" but everyone thinks they're the one loving more. You can't just give a hundred percent, you give five hundred percent. The other person thinks they do, too. And both of you still feel the other's not giving enough. Here's a love gift.

BECCA: Twizzlers! A pound of them!

SUSAN: You'll work your way through them in no time. *(She takes out a newspaper.)* And the paper.

BECCA: Thanks, but you keep it.

SUSAN: You read it already?

BECCA: No, and that's the point. I don't want to stress out. I'm off all social media. All of it. No more bad news.

SUSAN: If you're feeling anxious we should call the Doctor.

BECCA: It's just me freaking, thinking about this world a baby comes into. Which is ridiculous, because this is totally your decision. I'm just the stork.

SUSAN: But what's the alternative? We give up and stop having children because we're afraid? You know what made me first think I wanted to be a Mother? A nine-thousand dollar sofa.

BECCA: A couch?

SUSAN: When it's at Fendi Maison they call it a sofa.

BECCA: Got it.

SUSAN: I was lighting a decadently priced living room set and I noticed how the light bounced off this sofa. It almost glowed, this gleaming, spotless leather. Five years ago, if I saw that sofa I would have killed for it. But this time I imagined it with a big scrape across it made by a wizard's wand and stains from a leaky magic marker that wouldn't come out. Things that would scare off anybody who could buy it. But I thought it was perfect. The stains and scrapes meant some little kid was actually playing on it and that his parents loved their kid more than their furniture. I didn't want the couch. I wanted the kid. A kid who maybe, someday will be important to this world. Or his kid or his kid's kid. You're right about the world. Even on good days it's scary. But what if the one person who could make a difference is never born?

(SUSAN *picks up the early pregnancy test and hands it to* BECCA. BECCA *reluctantly takes.* SUSAN *takes a breath. Looks at her watch. Picks up the newspaper. She looks at the front page, shakes her head. Turns to another page. Then another. Finally, she stuffs the paper back in the bag. Sound of the bathroom door closing.* BECCA *enters, looks at* SUSAN *who stares back expectantly.* BECCA *shakes her head "yes".* SUSAN *screams;* BECCA *screams, the women hug each other)*

SUSAN/BECCA: I'M PREGNANT/ WE'RE HAVING A BABY!/YES/OH MY GOD!

(Blackout)

Scene 8

(Merrit home—the present)

(Lights up on DETECTIVE VALEZ *and* DETECTIVE DIXON*)*

DETECTIVE VALEZ: We did a full sweep. There's nothing we like for the murder weapon.

DETECTIVE DIXON: Back yard?

DETECTIVE VALEZ: The lawn's smooth as a golf course. No signs of digging. All the trash in the neighborhood's been checked out and they're working the sewers now.

DETECTIVE DIXON: You say there's a safe?

DETECTIVE VALEZ: In the den.

DETECTIVE DIXON: If the weapon's around seven pounds it could have been dumped anywhere. There's that pond he would have passed on his way home.

DETECTIVE VALEZ: We're saying "him" already?

DETECTIVE DIXON: Who do you make for it?

DETECTIVE VALEZ: Nobody, yet. There's this thing I heard about in the Academy: it's called an Open Mind.

DETECTIVE DIXON: When I was in school they told us, "First thing you do is listen to your gut."

DETECTIVE VALEZ: With the size of your gut, do you have a choice?

(DETECTIVE VALEZ' *cell phone beeps. She walks away to talk.* STRUTT *enters.*)

STRUTT: How's treasure hunting?

DETECTIVE DIXON: You call the Merrits?

STRUTT: They're right behind me.

DETECTIVE DIXON: You want to make some coffee?

STRUTT: Soon as your Bundt cake's done.

(MARTIN *and* SUSAN *enter.*)

SUSAN: Why didn't you tell us about this?

MARTIN: You could have called us!

STRUTT: They don't have to.

(DETECTIVE DIXON *hands* SUSAN *a warrant.*)

MARTIN: What's that?

STRUTT: Their warrant.

DETECTIVE VALEZ: We need one of you to open your safe.

SUSAN: *(To* STRUTT*)* Do I have to do this?

STRUTT: If you don't they'll open it themselves.

(SUSAN *looks at* MARTIN, *who shrugs.*)

SUSAN: *(To* DETECTIVE VALEZ*)* This way.

(SUSAN *and* DETECTIVE VALEZ *exit.*)

DETECTIVE DIXON: Martin—can I call you Martin?

MARTIN: No.

DETECTIVE DIXON: Have you been to Israel?

MARTIN: Many times. I've been going for years.

DETECTIVE DIXON: When was your last visit?

MARTIN: I'm bad with dates. I'm trying to remember.

DETECTIVE DIXON: Does last year March 3 to April 17 sound right?

MARTIN: I can check.

DETECTIVE DIXON: They're the dates on your passport.

MARTIN: Then why ask if you know already? Why would I hide going to Israel?

DETECTIVE DIXON: I'm wondering the same thing.

(SUSAN *and* DETECTIVE VALEZ *re-enter.*DETECTIVE VALEZ, *she shakes her head "no".*)

STRUTT: Why don't you just tell us what you're looking for?

DETECTIVE DIXON: Mrs Merrit, when's your last time in Israel?

SUSAN: I haven't gone in years.

DETECTIVE DIXON: 2014?

SUSAN: That sounds right.

STRUTT: Are you hustling Holy Land tours?

DETECTIVE DIXON: (*To* MARTIN) What's "Meleki"? (*Pronounces it "MA-LEK-EYE"*)

MARTIN: (*Correcting him*) "Meleki."(*MA-LEK-EE*) It's a stone only found in Israel. It was used building most of the Old City, which dates back to Solomon. The Western Wall's made of it.

DETECTIVE DIXON: You do work in the Old City?

MARTIN: My digging site is in Sephoris, a few miles outside it. We're excavating a Temple that might go back to 100 B C.

DETECTIVE DIXON: This stone was used to build it?

MARTIN: And what's left of Sephoris.

DETECTIVE DIXON: The autopsy says what killed Becca was a heavy rock. There were sediments found in Becca's skull. You bring back any "Melekee"?

MARTIN: No.

(MARTIN *looks at* STRUTT. *She nods permission to continue*)

MARTIN: I couldn't if I wanted to. Anything we find, after it's catalogued, we turn over to the Museum of Israel. That's not just our policy, it's Israeli law.

STRUTT: You didn't find anything to contradict that, did you? We'd be at the station if you did.

DETECTIVE VALEZ: Mrs. Merrit, do you have anything made of this stone?

SUSAN: Absolutely not.

DETECTIVE VALEZ: Not even jewelry?

SUSAN: No. You heard Martin. It's illegal.

DETECTIVE DIXON: So Becca was killed by an illegal rock nobody ever heard of. But you two.

STRUTT: This dig's over.

DETECTIVE DIXON: Forensics found a trace of blood on the inside door knob that wasn't Becca's. *(To* SUSAN*)* Whoever used it could have cut a finger on the rock.

STRUTT: The disappearing rock.

DETECTIVE VALEZ: We need blood samples from you both.

STRUTT: They're voluntary?

DETECTIVE DIXON: For now. *(To* MARTIN*)* Why does Roberto Trainor have it in for you?

SUSAN: Who?

STRUTT: *(To* MARTIN*)* Martin—

MARTIN: It's fine. He works for me at the Museum. He's angry because I'm not extending his contract.

DETECTIVE DIXON: He says you're the one with a temper. You smashed a plaster cast he made right in front of him?

MARTIN: I was tossing it in the garbage and missed. The mold he made was unusable. It was his third try.

DETECTIVE DIXON: Did Trainor know about your Surrogate?

MARTIN: We don't talk. Just throw things.

DETECTIVE DIXON: Good. That might explain it.

MARTIN: What?

DETECTIVE DIXON: He seemed to enjoy telling me that he didn't see you all afternoon.

MARTIN: He wouldn't have. I loaned him to paleontology. I don't trust him with my work. Did you ask anyone else?

DETECTIVE DIXON: Yeah. You're not a memorable guy.

MARTIN: I was in my office most of the day. Doors closed.

STRUTT: You want to talk more, Detectives, come back with an arrest warrant.

MARTIN: This is such a waste of time! Instead of harassing us, go find the person who did this.

DETECTIVE DIXON: We will.

STRUTT: Good-bye, Detectives.

DETECTIVE DIXON: As Sister Lynn Mary said every day at the three o'clock bell: 'It's been a little bit of heaven right

here on earth being with you today.'

(DETECTIVE DIXON *and VELEZ exit.*)

STRUTT: Did you ever see a rock like that in her apartment? Martin? Susan?

(They look at each other)

STRUTT: Anybody?

Scene 9

(Outside MARTIN and SUSAN's home

DETECTIVE VALEZ: Paul called. The Adoption Bureau wants to see us. They close at 4:30.

DETECTIVE DIXON: Go. The last thing I want around here is an open mind.

DETECTIVE VALEZ: It looks real this time. Don't wish us luck, you'll jinx it.

Scene 10

(Inside MARTIN and SUSAN's home)

MARTIN: Becca was interested in archeology. Maybe she found a piece. I'm sure you can buy it on the dark web.

STRUTT: Susan?

SUSAN: I have no idea.

STRUTT: Then get one, both of you. Until they get some answers they won't look hard at anybody else.

(STRUTT leaves. MARTIN puts his hand on SUSAN'S shoulder)

SUSAN: Don't touch me. *(She exits.)*

Scene 11

(BECCA's *apartment—before the murder*)

(*Lights up on* BECCA. MARTIN *steps into the scene carrying a box*)

BECCA: Guess what?

MARTIN: What?

BECCA: I put music on today and I felt her dancing.

MARTIN: It's too early for that, isn't it?

BECCA: Not for this baby. She was boogying.

MARTIN: "She"? Do you know something we don't?

BECCA: This far ahead of the developmental curve, she's got to be a she. What'cha got?

MARTIN: (*Puts down box*) Some pictures of the site we're excavating. If you get bored you might want to take a look.

BECCA: Wow.

MARTIN: Was that a "what a nerd" "wow"?

BECCA: It's short for "Wowee".

MARTIN: That's better.

(BECCA *joins* MARTIN *and looks through the pictures.*)

MARTIN: Teams have been excavating since '85. We're uncovering a whole city. This is a Roman Villa, check out the tile floor. See here, in the middle? The room was designed so guests could party around the mosaic but still see it.

BECCA: "Partying" means staring at floor tile?

MARTIN: Check it out. I've got a better picture. Here.

BECCA: She's so beautiful. She looks alive.

MARTIN: They made it with tiny tiles called tesserae. The smaller they are, the more detail they make. Probably used a thousand tesserae. More. It's incredible artistry. They call her the "Madonna of the Galilee".

BECCA: The Virgin Mary? She can't be.

MARTIN: No halo?

BECCA: Not just that. Isn't that Dionysius behind her?

MARTIN: Good eye. I know Archeologists who would need a week to figure that out. It could be Dionysius. Chronologically, it couldn't be Mary. Art Scholars think she's a Roman figure, probably Venus. Historians think she could be the wife of a rich man who owned the Villa.

BECCA: I'll stick with Mary. *(Turns page)* Is this an orgy?

MARTIN: It's the Festival of Lupercus, the Roman God of Fertility. *(Looks closer)* Yes, it's an orgy.

BECCA: Sex! It's the only time I miss Sam.

MARTIN: Sam's your Professor?

BECCA: Yeah. How long does it take to get a degree in archeology?

MARTIN: What? Where'd that come from? What happened to musical theater?

BECCA: That was a phase.

MARTIN: And your M B A?

BECCA: Did Lara Croft need an M B A? I want to do something important, not just make money. Change something besides my mind. Learn your past and you learn your future, right?

MARTIN: You think? Susan thinks I love the past to avoid the present. I'm not very good at real life.

BECCA: You are. I'll prove it. *(Jumping up)* Here's the future. Stand up. *(She turns on the music.)* Give me your hand.

(Still dancing, BECCA *puts* MARTIN's *hand on her belly.)*

BECCA: Can you feel her?

MARTIN: No.

BECCA: Wait! Wait! Wait! *(Bigger dance moves)* Now?

*(*MARTIN's *expression changes.)*

MARTIN: I think…maybe..

BECCA: Right?

MARTIN: I do! Definitely!

BECCA: Go, Baby! Dance with Daddy!

(Now MARTIN'S *dancing, too.* BECCA *dances right up to* MARTIN. *Too close)*

BECCA: Isn't it awesome?

MARTIN: For the first time I really believe it's going to happen.

BECCA: How's it feel?

MARTIN: *(Tentative)* Good.

BECCA: That's a half-ass "good".

MARTIN: No, it's great. I guess I'm in shock.

BECCA: Scared?

MARTIN: A little. It's really happening.

BECCA: Oh yeah. How 'bout a drink to celebrate?

MARTIN: Not your healthy green stuff.

BECCA: Hold on. *(She goes into the kitchen, returns with a glass and a bottle of rum.)* Better?

MARTIN: You're not drinking that—

BECCA: Not now. But after I have this baby I'm coming home to Captain Morgan.

(BECCA *pours for* MARTIN, *takes her green juice*)

BECCA: A toast. To your daughter?

MARTIN: To my daughter.

BECCA: How about your father?

MARTIN: Dad? On behalf of your granddaughter, I am so glad you're gone.

BECCA: That's really cold.

MARTIN: It is, sorry, but now I can't stop thinking: What if I have a kid and I turn into my Father? We had nothing in common. Nothing. He judged a man by what football team's flag he had on his lawn and whether he washed his car every week. When I told him I wanted to study archeology he said, "Go dig up the rocks in the backyard so they don't break the lawn mower."

BECCA: Your Father must have been proud, then, when you went to Israel.

MARTIN: No. Why?

BECCA: You were digging up rocks.

(BECCA *and* MARTIN *both laugh.*)

MARTIN: That's true. So now I think, 'What if I have a kid like him'? Or me.

BECCA: If she's like you it's a lucky baby.

MARTIN: That's nice of you.

BECCA: I mean it. But now it's going to look like I'm trying to work you.

MARTIN: "Work" me? Why?

BECCA: After the baby's born, can I come with you on your next Sephoris dig?

MARTIN: Seriously?

BECCA: You're doing something important! And I'll find out if archeology is for me.

MARTIN: We only take archeology students.

BECCA: I'll sign up for classes.

MARTIN: I need to think about this.

BECCA: Why? You trust me enough to carry your baby.

MARTIN: I do, but—

BECCA: You like me. Don't you? Like me?

MARTIN: Of course.

BECCA: Really like me.

MARTIN: I said I did.

BECCA: Is that the problem?

MARTIN: I'm not sure what you mean.

BECCA: It means…take me.

(BECCA *takes* MARTIN'*s hand, puts it back on her belly.*)

BECCA: Feel anything?

MARTIN: Yeah.

(BECCA *puts her hand over* MARTIN'*s.*)

BECCA: Me too.

Scene 12

(Police station—the present

(DETECTIVE VALEZ *shows photos on her phone to* DETECTIVE DIXON*)*

DETECTIVE DIXON: This is one seriously cute kid.

DETECTIVE VALEZ: I know it's impossible, but she's got Paul's eyes.

DETECTIVE DIXON: You're right. It's impossible.

DETECTIVE VALEZ: I'm taking maternity leave.

DETECTIVE DIXON: Good! But you'll miss me.

DETECTIVE VALEZ: Sorry, I have another baby to take care of.

DETECTIVE DIXON: I never saw you smile like you just did.

DETECTIVE VALEZ: I never felt this way before. You've held a baby, right?

DETECTIVE DIXON: I don't remember.

DETECTIVE VALEZ: She looks up at me and I think, this life is in my hands. It really is. All she has is me to feed her, protect her and make sure she grows up smart and strong and happy. Happy, most of all.

DETECTIVE DIXON: How's Fire Guy?

DETECTIVE VALEZ: Over the moon. He told me last night he had been afraid. He said he loved me so much he didn't know if he had enough love in him for a baby, too. But when he saw her, he felt his chest fill up with love he didn't even know he had.

DETECTIVE DIXON: Even though she's adopted?

(DETECTIVE VALEZ *decides whether to be annoyed at the question. No*)

DETECTIVE VALEZ: This baby was meant to be ours, no matter if she came from inside of me or from outside. *(Pause)* How do you like the name "Sushauna"?

(Long pause)

DETECTIVE DIXON: The blood spatter report came in.

DETECTIVE VALEZ: And?

DETECTIVE DIXON: I don't get it. Susan Merrit says she found Becca behind the front door. She pushed her way in.

DETECTIVE VALEZ: Right.

DETECTIVE DIXON: But the blood spatter indicates the victim was hit about ten feet from the couch.

DETECTIVE VALEZ: Okay.

DETECTIVE DIXON: Becca's phone was on the couch's end table. Merrit picked it up to call.

DETECTIVE VALEZ: Which means Becca crawled past that phone toward the front door.

DETECTIVE DIXON: Why? She wasn't going to run for help in her shape. Why didn't she call 9-1-1?

DETECTIVE VALEZ: Anybody else confirm Martin Merrit was at the museum?

DETECTIVE DIXON: Two saw him late morning and mid-afternoon. His door was closed most of the day.

DETECTIVE VALEZ: Which gives us nothing. And her?

DETECTIVE DIXON: We've got her at Trader Joes about twenty minutes from Becca. It times out.

(The phone rings, DETECTIVE DIXON *picks it up)*

DETECTIVE DIXON: Dixon.

*(*DETECTIVE VALEZ *picks up a paper on* DETECTIVE DIXON'S *and inspects it)*

DETECTIVE DIXON: Uh huh… Okay…wait, slow down. *(To* DETECTIVE VALEZ*)* It's the lab. *(On phone)* Explain that again, like you're talking to a normal person… Stop, I'll be right there with my expert.

DETECTIVE VALEZ: What "expert"?

DETECTIVE DIXON: You pass high school biology?

DETECTIVE VALEZ: Yeah.

DETECTIVE DIXON: Let's go, Expert.

Scene 13

(Elsewhere/Surgery waiting room—elsewhere)

(Light on BECCA *in an examination gown)*

BECCA: I decided to find the Virgin Mary. If anyone had answers she would. If there were answers and if there was a "Virgin". I always thought her story was pretty sketchy. Like a gullibility test. An Angel comes to Mary and says "You're going to give birth to the Son of God". And she says, "Why not? I'll be pregnant, even without having sex!" Is that the worst deal of all time? And how does she get pregnant? Not just by a Ghost, but a Holy Ghost. Okay, she has the kid. Then Joseph, who got the world's second worst deal, says let's get out of town, this is really awkward. So, Jesus grows up and starts treating Mary like she's help. They take a Family Vacation, He runs away, and when they track him down in the Temple, He tells her to back off, He's all about "His Father's Business." That's the last straw for Joseph—he's out of the Bible. Jesus grows up and gets even worse. Mary can't even ask for a favor, she has to beg for it: 'Jesus, they're out of wine. This whole wedding reception's going down suck street.' What does he say? "That's not my problem, Woman." Woman, right? No Mom, Mother, Mommy. And on top of it, she's still a virgin. So, if I found Mary I wanted to say, "This Virgin thing? What's in it for you?" And then Mary found me.

Scene 14

(The fertility clinic—before the murder)

(Lights up on MARTIN *and* SUSAN *sitting on chairs in the doctor's office.* MARTIN *flips through a magazine,* SUSAN *waits nervously)*

SUSAN: She's been in there forever.

MARTIN: No.

SUSAN: Maybe she was just spotting.

MARTIN: That's why we're here. To find out.

SUSAN: Why couldn't we stay with her?

MARTIN: Because we're not Doctors?

SUSAN: You really felt the baby move?

MARTIN: Dance.

SUSAN: And that was only a week ago.

MARTIN: Less than that.

SUSAN: *(Rising)* I'll ask someone how she is.

MARTIN: Susan, sit.

SUSAN: Will you stop being so calm?

MARTIN: *(To* SUSAN*)* Did I tell you I love you today?

SUSAN: No. But you better.

MARTIN: You bet.

*(*BECCA *enters, devastated.)*

BECCA: I am so sorry.

SUSAN: Oh, Becca!

*(*MARTIN *and* SUSAN *rush to* BECCA*.)*

BECCA: I did everything they told me to. I swear.

MARTIN: Of course you did. It's not your fault.

SUSAN: Shhhh. Shhh. Honey, it's all right.

MARTIN: It just wasn't meant to be.

SUSAN: Let's get you home. You must be exhausted.

MARTIN: What can we do? We can stop for something. Whatever you want.

BECCA: I just want to go to bed.

MARTIN: You got it. I'll bring the car around. *(To* SUSAN*)* Are you okay? *(He exits.)*

BECCA: I'll go change.

SUSAN: Sit.

*(*BECCA *and* SUSAN *sit.)*

*(*BECCA *hugs her.* SUSAN *rocks her gently)*

BECCA: I feel like such a failure.

SUSAN: That's how I feel, honey.

BECCA: You shouldn't.

SUSAN: Neither should you. It's okay, Becca. It really is. Things happen.

(Pause. BECCA *and* SUSAN *rock.)*

SUSAN: So don't worry. We'll try again. Right?

Scene 15A

*(Police station/*BECCA*'s apartment/*SUSAN *and* MARTIN*'s home,* STRUTT*'s home—after the murder. Police station)*

*(*DETECTIVE DIXON *looks up from his report.)*

DETECTIVE DIXON: Run this by me again. "Amniotic Fluid"?

DETECTIVE VALEZ: It surrounds the embryo and protects it.

DETECTIVE DIXON: Okay.

DETECTIVE VALEZ: They did amniotic testing on Becca only three days before she aborted. Since Becca had a miscarriage the first time she was pregnant, when she got pregnant again, they tested her. It detects if the parents have a significant genetic risk.

DETECTIVE DIXON: But it says right here the genes weren't a problem. So the baby was fine, right?

DETECTIVE VALEZ: Their genes weren't. Keep reading.

DETECTIVE DIXON: *(Pause)* This is impossible.

Scene 15B

(MARTIN and SUSAN's home—after the murder

(MARTIN *enters a room where* SUSAN *is sketching)*

MARTIN: Can we talk?

SUSAN: I can.

MARTIN: Why are you so angry?

SUSAN: Do you remember Bobby Nichols?

MARTIN: Sure. You went out with him.

SUSAN: We almost got engaged.

MARTIN: Okay.

SUSAN: One night I got up and saw he left his computer on.

MARTIN: You read his email?

SUSAN: That's what he was angry about. Me, I got a little upset when I read a subject line that said, "Hello Beautiful". An old girlfriend was coming to town and wanted to get together.

MARTIN: He said he would?

SUSAN: I didn't read that far. I stopped when I saw the email was three days old. He hadn't told me about it for three days.

MARTIN: But you didn't know if he was going to meet her.

SUSAN: That wasn't the point. He shouldn't have kept it from me. Not telling me was the same thing as lying. He couldn't understand that. Do you?

MARTIN: Why are you telling me this?

SUSAN: Sometimes I think I overreacted. That I should have taken a breath, given him a second chance to say more. This is yours, Martin. Tell me.

Scene 15C

*(Police station/*MERRIT *home)*

DETECTIVE DIXON: Somebody's lying.

DETECTIVE VALEZ: Or Becca lied to all of them.

DETECTIVE DIXON: Can't ask her.

DETECTIVE VALEZ: So now what?

DETECTIVE DIXON: Talk to the Medical Examiner. Start again. And get smarter.

SUSAN: Martin?

MARTIN: I don't know what you want me to tell you.

SUSAN: The truth. When's the last time you saw Becca?

MARTIN: When? The night before she died. And then it was your turn.

SUSAN: The night before she died?

MARTIN: Yes. Does that matter?

SUSAN: It matters to me because you're lying to me. To me, your best friend. Last chance, Martin. When is the last time you saw her?

MARTIN: I just told you, Susan! If you think I slept with Becca, you're wrong. Totally, completely wrong. I love you!

SUSAN: I wish I could believe that.

MARTIN: Susan, what do you want me to do, here?

SUSAN: Go upstairs and pack.

Scene 15D

(STRUTT's *home*)

STRUTT: *(Picking up phone)* Strutt.

(Lights up on MARTIN*)*

MARTIN: *(Panicked)* It's Martin. I need to talk to you.

STRUTT: It's late, Martin. Can't it wait 'till tomorrow?

MARTIN: It's about the day Becca died. There are things I didn't tell you.

STRUTT: Stop! No more on the phone. Meet me at my office. Now.

Scene 15E

(BECCA's *apartment—night after the miscarriage—flashback*)

(BECCA *pages through one of* MARTIN's *books.*)

(Sound of knock)

BECCA: Come in.

(PROFESSOR SAMANTHA SUTTON *does.*)

BECCA: I didn't think you'd come.

(SAM steps in.)

SAM: Of course I would. Becca? What's wrong?

BECCA: Everything.

(BECCA goes into SAM's arms.)

BECCA: I can't do anything right.

SAM: You can. I know you can. Sometimes, it takes time to understand what the right thing is.

BECCA: So, tell me, Sam.

(SAM kisses BECCA, BECCA returns it.)

(Blackout)

(Music: something like You Better You Bet by The Who)

END OF ACT ONE

ACT TWO

Scene 1

(Somewhere past time)

(Lights up on BECCA)

BECCA: Mary doesn't look like she does in white people's bibles. Her skin is olive and her dark hair is tied back with a streak of red where it's parted. But it's her. You know that, for sure. Hearing her voice, it felt like I was floating in warm water. "Becca", she said, "You have a question." "Yes, yes! I want to know who murdered me!" "Oh." Mary seemed almost disappointed. "There are so many bigger questions."

Scene 2

(Bar—the present)

(Lights up on DETECTIVE VALEZ carrying two drinks to a table, handing one to STRUTT.)

STRUTT: A cop walks into a bar and buys a lawyer a drink. This is a joke, right? Cheers.

DETECTIVE VALEZ: Salud.

STRUTT: Okay. Small talk over. What do you want, Detective? You know I can't discuss the Merrit case.

DETECTIVE VALEZ: Sure. This is something else. I hear you used to work Family Court.

STRUTT: When Giants walked the earth.

DETECTIVE VALEZ: My husband and I just adopted a baby girl.

STRUTT: Congratulations.

DETECTIVE VALEZ: They took her away from us last night. Her Grandmother got a court order; she says she had no idea her Daughter gave her up.

STRUTT: Did the Mother sign off on the adoption?

DETECTIVE VALEZ: Yeah, but the Grandmother says she's a crack head who didn't know what she was signing. Social Services came for our daughter last night. They said Grandma claimed custody. How can she do that?

STRUTT: What do you know about Grandma?

DETECTIVE VALEZ: She has no record. But both her kids do.

STRUTT: Do they live with her?

DETECTIVE VALEZ: I don't know.

STRUTT: Find out. If they're out of the house it won't matter.

DETECTIVE VALEZ: We have to get her back. We love this girl.

STRUTT: How long have you had her?

DETECTIVE VALEZ: Almost a week.

STRUTT: You don't have an appeal, Detective.

DETECTIVE VALEZ: Wait! I found the Grandmother's address. She lives in a falling down house in Riverhead. The Department uses Riverhead like a dump for cops they're forcing into retirement. If the grandmother raises Sushauna she won't stand a chance.

STRUTT: You don't know that.

DETECTIVE VALEZ: I've been on the job six years.

STRUTT: I used to have one chin.

DETECTIVE VALEZ: Her Grandmother's all of 33.
I knocked on her door today to tell her there's been
even more robberies than usual in her neighborhood,
so keep her doors locked.

STRUTT: I'll assume you weren't in uniform, since, if
you were, you could be put up on criminal charges.

DETECTIVE VALEZ: She wouldn't let me in.

STRUTT: Did she know you adopted her
granddaughter?

DETECTIVE VALEZ: They don't get that information. I
had to threaten her to open the door and even then she
kept the chain on.

STRUTT: A cop hater in Riverhead? Who knew?

DETECTIVE VALEZ: I could see into her living room.
She's got cartons piled up, mostly electronics. They've
got to be stolen or fell of a truck. And I guarantee she's
got guns or drugs.

STRUTT: You shouldn't have been there. You saw
nothing.

DETECTIVE VALEZ: What if someone called in an
anonymous tip: If Grandma has a record, can I get her
back?

STRUTT: Detective—

DETECTIVE VALEZ: Aleece.

STRUTT: Aleece. There are so many things wrong here.
Do you really want to put your career on the line?

DETECTIVE VALEZ: I love this girl.

STRUTT: And she loves you, too. A whole week's worth.

DETECTIVE VALEZ: Do you have a child?

STRUTT: *(A moment pause)* No.

DETECTIVE VALEZ: Then you have no idea what it feels like.

STRUTT: Forget feelings for now and think with your head.

DETECTIVE VALEZ: You think I became a cop because I used my head? I have a Master's in Education. I could have sat behind a desk instead of thanking God every day I don't get shot. How long would she serve if she was busted?

STRUTT: Could be no time. Grandma's first time, two- or three-year's probation. But to get that she'll have to give names. The more relatives who have records the better

DETECTIVE VALEZ: That can happen.

STRUTT: Aleece. How far do you want to push this?

DETECTIVE VALEZ: Until I get my kid back.

(STRUTT finishes her drink, puts the empty glass down in front of DETECTIVE VALEZ)

STRUTT: You want my advice? Let it go.

DETECTIVE VALEZ: I can't.

STRUTT: Then buy me another drink.

Scene 3

(BECCA's apartment—before the murder)

(Lights up revealing SAM and BECCA, post lovemaking, sharing a carton of Cherry Garcia ice cream.)

BECCA: You know who I saw at the Fertility Clinic?

SAM: Who?

BECCA: Your Ex. Trish. Why'd you drop her? She age out?

SAM: Our age difference only matters to you when we're out of bed. One question.

BECCA: Go.

SAM: Did you get pregnant just to hurt me?

BECCA: No.

SAM: You didn't want to have our baby, why would you have theirs?

BECCA: I needed money to stay in school. I already knew so much about all this, it seemed like a good idea. I shouldn't have called you.

SAM: I'm glad you did.

BECCA: I freaked out. I shouldn't have involved you. And you're not involved.

SAM: I'm here, aren't I? Look, I can't help the way I feel—

BECCA: And you can't stop telling me.

SAM: I waited my whole life to feel like this—

BECCA: You want me too much!

SAM: Why is that wrong?

BECCA: It makes me think less of you.

SAM: Please. No Thornton Wilder! You can't measure love! And even if one person feels more strongly, it's still love! I know what settling is, I've done it. But I can't now. I wish I could. When you walked into the lecture hall the first day I felt fluttery. I really did. I said, please God, let her be dumb as a rock. Then you raised your hand to tell me I spelled "corporea" wrong on the blackboard and I thought, Goddamn it, my life just changed. So many things stopped mattering. My age, my job, my dignity. Only one thing was important.

Finding that person who's the reason to wake up every morning.

BECCA: Violins, please.

SAM: I want you in my life. Even if it's as a friend.

BECCA: Really. Just as "a friend"?

SAM: Not "just". A real friend is rare. A lot rarer than a lover.

BECCA: I always feel I'm still in school with you.

SAM: So far, you're failing.

BECCA: They want me to try again. Carrying their baby.

(Pause)

SAM: Why would you do that?

BECCA: Money—

SAM: I can give you that.

BECCA: I'd like to succeed at something. And I like the husband.

SAM: "Like".

BECCA: He's an archeologist and he's just so passionate about it.

SAM: Is he passionate about you?

BECCA: I like what he does. I like that he gets excited. I'm going with him to Israel to work on his dig.

SAM: He agreed to that?

BECCA: He will.

SAM: If you have his baby?

BECCA: I'm not bribing him.

SAM: What about his wife? Remember her?

BECCA: She'll have the baby to take care of.

SAM: And you'll take care of her husband. Does he know you're—

BECCA: Bi-Gay-Straight? I don't know what I am.

SAM: This semester, the school recognized sixty-three gender categories and there's a new classification every week. I can send you the emails.

BECCA: Martin likes me. He thinks I'm smart. I'm going to do it. No matter what you say. *(She waits for the argument.)*

SAM: Do you even want to hear what I'd say?

BECCA: Yes.

SAM: I say you're right. You should.

BECCA: Should what? Go with him or have his baby?

SAM: Both.

BECCA: Really?

SAM: Really.

BECCA: Thank you!

(Excited, BECCA *hugs* SAM.)

SAM: See that? Am I a good friend or what?

(Spontaneously, BECCA *kisses* SAM.)

Scene 4

*(*MARTIN *and* SUSAN's *home—after the murder)*

*(*DETECTIVE DIXON *and* DETECTIVE VALEZ *wait at the front door)*

DETECTIVE DIXON: *(Tentative)* How you doing, okay?

DETECTIVE VALEZ: How do I answer that? You ask if I'm okay then tell me I'm okay. No, I'm not okay.

DETECTIVE DIXON: Every cop in the precinct's keeping an eye on that house. You'll get your kid back.

DETECTIVE VALEZ: Right. We'll see.

DETECTIVE DIXON: You wait. She'll screw up, or her family will. Don't you do it for them.

DETECTIVE VALEZ: How many times have you seen our side screw up?

(Sound of MARTIN *and* SUSAN'*s doorbell)*

SUSAN: *(Opens the door)* Come in.

*(*DETECTIVE DIXON *and* DETECTIVE VALEZ *enter, see two suitcases)*

DETECTIVE DIXON: Who's going on vacation?

SUSAN: Martin has grant deadline. He's staying at a hotel in the city to save commuting time.

DETECTIVE DIXON: *(Not buying it)* Uh-huh.

DETECTIVE VALEZ: Is he home?

DETECTIVE DIXON: *(To* DETECTIVE VALEZ*)* Takes me an hour fifteen, maybe an hour thirty to get into the city.

SUSAN: *(Calls offstage)* Martin!

DETECTIVE DIXON: Some people work on the train.

MARTIN: *(Enters)* What now?

DETECTIVE VALEZ: Mrs Merrit, we've gotten more findings from the coroner's office.

DETECTIVE DIXON: How 'bout we all sit down?

MARTIN: This is my house. How about we don't and you tell us why you're here.

SUSAN: What did the Coroner's Office find?

DETECTIVE DIXON: We need another genetic sampling from you.

SUSAN: *(Confused)* From me? Why?

DETECTIVE VALEZ: We're just telling you what the lab's requested.

MARTIN: You want hers and not mine? Why? She was carrying our baby, it's our D N A.

SUSAN: I don't understand.

MARTIN: This is ridiculous. Who else's genes could it be? You're saying mine match—

DETECTIVE VALEZ: We didn't say that.

MARTIN: But she's the one who needs to be retested? Not me?

DETECTIVE DIXON: Correct.

SUSAN: *(Pause)* Are you're saying Martin fertilized someone else's egg?

DETECTIVE VALEZ: We're saying the State wants to retest.

SUSAN: What about Becca's D N A? Is hers a match?

DETECTIVE VALEZ: We don't have that information.

SUSAN: Of course you do. Wasn't her D N A part of the autopsy?

DETECTIVE DIXON: You said Becca broke up with a Professor she dated. What else did she mention?

SUSAN: Just that they had a bad breakup.

DETECTIVE DIXON: No name?

MARTIN: Sam. She mentioned the name "Sam".

SUSAN: That's right.

DETECTIVE DIXON: Sam Sutton?

MARTIN: I don't know his last name.

DETECTIVE VALEZ: "Her".

DETECTIVE DIXON: That's a masculine faux pas.

(DETECTIVE VALEZ's *phone goes off. She looks quickly, surprised. Concerned)*

DETECTIVE VALEZ: *(To* DETECTIVE DIXON*)* I'd better take this. *(She exits)*

DETECTIVE DIXON: The only "Sam" who taught her was Professor Samantha Sutton.

MARTIN: *(Surprised)* Oh.

DETECTIVE DIXON: That surprise you?

MARTIN: Not at all. It doesn't matter. We hired her to carry our baby. She did her job.

SUSAN: Until she killed it.

DETECTIVE DIXON: You spent a lot of time together, though. Every other day, wasn't it?

MARTIN: That's what we decided on. Susan was there as much as I was. We alternated. She'd go one night, I'd go the next night.

SUSAN: Or day. Sometimes we stopped by during the day. Right, Martin?

MARTIN: Well, sure. Sometimes.

SUSAN: So tell him.

MARTIN: Tell him what?

SUSAN: What you never told me.

MARTIN: I'm not sure what you're talking about.

SUSAN: Your car, in Becca's parking lot. The day she was killed.

DETECTIVE DIXON: Really. Did I miss this? Or is it something you didn't tell me, either.

MARTIN: I didn't tell anyone because it's not what it seems.

DETECTIVE DIXON: It seems to me that if your car was there, you were too.

MARTIN: I was, but Becca wasn't. She wasn't home.

DETECTIVE DIXON: You checked.

MARTIN: Of course. But she was alive.

DETECTIVE DIXON: How did you know that?

MARTIN: I talked with her.

DETECTIVE DIXON: Even though she wasn't there.

MARTIN: I can explain *(To* SUSAN*)* you wouldn't let me explain.

DETECTIVE DIXON: How about you start by explaining it to me. We've got a long ride downtown, Marty.

MARTIN: *(To* SUSAN*)* Call Strutt.

SUSAN: Tell the truth. For once.

MARTIN: The truth? Thank God we didn't have a baby.

*(*SUSAN *slaps* MARTIN, *hard.)*

Scene 5

*(*STRUTT*'s office—after the murder)*

*(*DETECTIVE VALEZ *enters to* STRUTT*)*

STRUTT: I just sent over the stay order. I know the Clerk, she'll get it in front of Judge Howard first thing tomorrow morning.

DETECTIVE VALEZ: She's dead.

STRUTT: What?

DETECTIVE VALEZ: Sushauna's dead. You don't have to do...anything.

STRUTT: What happened?

DETECTIVE VALEZ: Not now.

STRUTT: Sit down. Just for a minute.

DETECTIVE VALEZ: *(Pause)* It's my fault.

STRUTT: What is?

DETECTIVE VALEZ: I heard from the Sgt. who brought in the Grandmother for questioning.

STRUTT: Her Grandmother killed her?

DETECTIVE VALEZ: Her Junkie Boyfriend did. When the Grandmother found out social services gave Sushauna to us she went in and raised hell. Corrine Monroe. She was family, it's her granddaughter. She would not leave until she left with her. The clerk at the desk didn't want to give her the baby. A white woman. Perfect. Corrine starts beating her with that. She's yelling loud enough to bring the Supervisor out, who brings them back to her office to talk. They argue and the whole office hears it. The baby's in good hands, a cop's hands! The Supervisor said they had no choice but to hand her over.

STRUTT: She was right.

DETECTIVE VALEZ: So, Corrine takes my baby home and tells her Junkie boyfriend they not only got the baby, but they took her from a cop! They got so high, made a crib out of a cardboard box and towels, like a dog's bed, then passed out. My baby started crying and wouldn't stop. Corrine held her, she still wouldn't stop. Then her Junkie yelled, "Shut that Cop Baby Up! Or I will". And he did. He grabbed her and shook her and kept shaking 'till she stopped crying. Becca did the right thing, you know. She did. It's better her baby wasn't born. She saved a kids from this world.

STRUTT: Maybe. Honey, what you do, what I do, we've seen hells most people can't imagine. No matter who you blame for Sushanna or try to make any sense of it you can't. The most you can know is that you don't know, no matter how smart you are. When Einstein was alive, way before your time, we thought he was a God. E = M c squared made sense of something, even though only scientists understood it. But if Einstein knew something, we knew something. He said, "God doesn't play dice with the universe", and we all felt better because someone finally found a real fact. But one blink later and we have Quantum Mechanics that puts him in mothballs and not a single Scientist can explain its laws, except that there are none. All they know is that they will change our way of thinking about time and space and prove we don't know anything. Again.

DETECTIVE VALEZ: What are you saying? We should stop thinking and watch the world burn?

STRUTT: We can't stop thinking. But we've got to keep going and think of anything around us that makes this all worth it. The people around us. The love you had for your baby, no matter how little time you had her.

DETECTIVE VALEZ: I can't do that to myself again. I do my job and that's enough. And when I think that my job means protecting her grandmother, I don't want to do that, either…

Scene 6

(*Police station—after the murder, Interview Room One*)

(DETECTIVE DIXON *enters with* SAM. *They take seats*)

DETECTIVE DIXON: More coffee?

SAM: This is good, thank you.

(BECCA *appears and watches.*)

DETECTIVE DIXON: Should I call you "Doctor Sutton", " Professor Sutton?"

SAM: Whatever you like.

DETECTIVE DIXON: How about "Sam"? Becca called you "Sam", didn't she?

SAM: She did.

DETECTIVE DIXON: Perfect. So, Sam, when Becca first met the Merrits, you two were no longer a couple.

SAM: That's right.

DETECTIVE DIXON: Did you see her after that?

SAM: Yes, twice. The first time was on campus, she was, maybe four weeks pregnant. The last time was a few days before she died.

DETECTIVE DIXON: Before somebody killed her.

SAM: Exactly.

DETECTIVE DIXON: Were these visits friendly?

SAM: Very, and I'm so glad of that. Being friends after a breakup isn't always easy.

DETECTIVE DIXON: Tell me about it. Did Becca ever talk to you about becoming a surrogate?

SAM: Not once.

DETECTIVE DIXON: That she thought about aborting?

SAM: Never.

DETECTIVE DIXON: Really. Isn't that strange? You'd think she would. You're a woman, a medical professional, a friend.

SAM: She didn't need to ask. She would have known my opinion.

DETECTIVE DIXON: What's that?

SAM: The cutoff in this state for an abortion is twenty-four weeks. It wasn't her child. I'd tell her to get it. Now. Before she ran out of time.

(Lights down on DETECTIVE DIXON, SAM *and* BECCA, *Lights up on* DETECTIVE VALEZ *and* MARTIN)

Scene 6B

(Interview Room Two—after the murder)

*(*DETECTIVE VALEZ *interviews* MARTIN*)*

MARTIN: I've told Dixon this.

DETECTIVE VALEZ: You got to her apartment at about noon.

MARTIN: About. *(Resigned to repeat himself)* I knocked, got no answer, so I called her.

Scene 6C

(Abortion clinic—before the murder)

(Lights up on BECCA, *very nervous, at the Clinic)*

BECCA: I went out, Martin! Okay? I can't sit in that apartment all day!

MARTIN: Of course not. I just wanted to see you.

BECCA: Why?

MARTIN: I've been thinking a lot about you wanting to come on the next dig.

BECCA: Okay.

MARTIN: I think I could use a Lara Croft.

BECCA: Really? Thank you, thank you!

MARTIN: No "Wowee"?

BECCA: To infinity.

*(*BECCA *realizes that after he learns of the abortion, he won't take her)*

MARTIN: Becca?

BECCA: But I can't go...

MARTIN: Why? You said you wanted to—

BECCA: I can't explain now. I changed my mind.

MARTIN: You *(changed your mind?)* ...Becca, what happened? Are you okay?

BECCA: Martin, don't come by tonight, I'll be out. And tell Susan, okay?

MARTIN: We won't be talking.

BECCA: I've got to go. Thank you, for, you know, for wanting me.

Scene 6D

(Interregation Room B—after the murder)

DETECTIVE VALEZ: Did you know where she was?

MARTIN: If I did she'd be alive.

Scene 6E

(Interrogation Room A—after the murder)

SAM: That night? I was at home.

DETECTIVE DIXON: You talk with anyone, see anyone?

SAM: No.

DETECTIVE DIXON: Watch T V?

SAM: I was reading.

DETECTIVE DIXON: Good for you.

SAM: So, I have no alibi, if that's what you're looking for.

DETECTIVE DIXON: Not a problem. But how about helping me out with a little biology? I don't know a lot about this amnio. I'm sure you do, being highly educated.

SAM: I'm happy to help.

DETECTIVE DIXON: Did Becca tell you they ran one of those tests on her? The amnio test?

SAM: No. She never mentioned that.

DETECTIVE DIXON: Tell me if I'm wrong here, but they say it points out the parents. Genes and all that. And it did. We know Martin was the Father.

SAM: Didn't you know that already?

DETECTIVE DIXON: Oh yeah. Where we're stuck now is with the Mother. The kid—

SAM: The fetus.

DETECTIVE DIXON: The "Fetus" has a "Mystery Mother". We've got no idea whose egg Martin fertilized, but it's not his wife's. How can that happen?

SAM: Easily enough. Women can save their eggs, they can be frozen and saved for whenever they want to use them. Fertility clinics make half their profits doing it. It could be any of a million eggs. But let me save you some time. I'm one of those women. I froze my eggs because if I choose to have a baby in the future, my age wouldn't prevent me from doing it.

DETECTIVE DIXON: Did Becca know this?

SAM: She did. But if you're thinking I gave Becca permission to use my eggs, you're wrong. I never would have given it.

Scene 6F

(Interrogation Room B—after the murder)

DETECTIVE VALEZ: Why did you let yourself into Becca's apartment when she wasn't there?

MARTIN: She sounded upset, on the phone. I was worried. I wanted to leave her…a present, I guess.

DETECTIVE VALEZ: The Meleki.

MARTIN: Right. The Meleki

Scene 6G

(Interrogation Room A—after the murder)

DETECTIVE DIXON: You never saw a rock in her apartment?

SAM: No.

DETECTIVE DIXON: Hold on. *(Checks notes)* Meleki. That's the kind of rock.

SAM: I don't even know what Meleki looks like.

DETECTIVE DIXON: Neither did I. You want to see?

SAM: *(Pause)* The meleki?

DETECTIVE DIXON: Yeah. We found it and tested the blood on it to be sure it was Becca's. Also for fingerprints. I'm sure you know this already, since you're all about science, but I had no idea that now you can pull prints from any surface. Wood, for instance, even rocks.

SAM: That's interesting. I didn't know.

DETECTIVE DIXON: Oh, yeah. The prints get harder to trust the more time goes by. Something about amino acids breaking apart. But it was early enough, we got a set. *(Takes her coffee mug)* Probably not as clear as your prints on this mug, but good enough to use as a match if we run them. Which we will. Unless you've got more to say.

Scene 7

(BECCA's apartment—*before the murder*)

(BECCA *screams at* SAM, *who enters the scene.*)

BECCA: Get out of here! Get out now!

SAM: Becca, calm down—

BECCA: You're a monster!

SAM: I'm not

BECCA: You switched eggs! You put your egg inside me. Of course! Trish at the Fertility Clinic! I wouldn't even know it happened if I didn't see the lab reports.

SAM: Becca, listen to me. We're going to be parents. We're going to have a beautiful baby and raise it like we always wanted.

BECCA: What you wanted!

SAM: We talked this out—

BECCA: It was just talk!

SAM: It was more than that! You said you weren't ready yet. I froze my eggs for you!

BECCA: I never asked you to.

SAM: We. Made. Plans.

BECCA: And then we broke up!

SAM: And then YOU called ME! You wanted me back in your life! You know you did!

BECCA: Listen to yourself! This is crazy! Don't you think Martin and Susan would have found out?

SAM: What if they did? Do you think THEY'D want our baby? Of course they wouldn't! And I'm her Mother!

BECCA: Who'd be arrested!

SAM: For what? By the time anyone figured that out we could be anywhere in the world! Anywhere you want!

BECCA: No!

SAM: We were together almost two years! You said you loved me! You can have a baby, someday. I can't! You owe me this!

BECCA: A baby?

SAM: You owe me!

BECCA: I DON'T OWE YOU ANYTHING!

SAM: If I can't have you I'll have my baby, who comes from you.

BECCA: Just go. Get away from me.

SAM: You agreed to this!

BECCA: You are sick.

SAM: YOU AGREED!

BECCA: GET OUT!

SAM: THE BABY IS MINE!

BECCA: THE BABY IS DEAD!

(SAM *is stunned.*)

BECCA: I got an abortion.

SAM: No.

BECCA: Of course I did.

SAM: How could you? Why?

BECCA: Because it was part of you! I will go to the police if I ever see you again! You think I could let you raise any baby? Never. Get out. You disgust me. Thank God you'll never be a Mother!

(BECCA *turns from her and goes into the kitchen.* SAM, *furious, picks up the meleki.*)

(*Blackout*)

Scene 8

(Interrogation Room A)

(Lights up on DETECTIVE DIXON *as* SAM *returns.* DETECTIVE DIXON *is looking up from his notes)*

DETECTIVE DIXON: How many times did you hit her?

SAM: I don't know. It happened so fast. I didn't think.

DETECTIVE DIXON: *(Pause)* Tell me. What does it look like?

SAM: What does what look like?

DETECTIVE DIXON: Meleki. Just curious. I've never seen a piece.

SAM: You said you found… *(She realizes she's been caught. She puts her head down)*

*(*DETECTIVE DIXON *mirandizes her in a surprisingly gentle way)*

DETECTIVE DIXON: I'm charging you with the murder of Becca Connor. You've got the right to remain silent. Do you understand this?

SAM: Yes.

DETECTIVE DIXON: Anything you say can and will be used against you in a court of law. Do you understand this?

SAM: Detective? Did you ever meet the love of your life?

DETECTIVE DIXON: No. I guess I never did.

SAM: You're a lucky guy.

(Lights fade on DETECTIVE DIXON *and* SAM, *lights up on the station, where* DETECTIVE VALEZ *is doing paperwork.)*

Scene 9

(Police station—office—the present)

(DET. DETECTIVE DIXON enters to DETECTIVE VALEZ, at her desk)

DETECTIVE DIXON: Go home. Knock off early.

DETECTIVE VALEZ: Good to see you, too. I'll stick around, she should be here soon.

DETECTIVE DIXON: Right. *(Pause)* How you doing? *(Catching himself)* You're not okay.

DETECTIVE VALEZ: Paul and I took ourselves off the list for adoption.

DETECTIVE DIXON: Uh huh.

DETECTIVE VALEZ: He fought me. But I told him, with my job, his job, we do enough. You know?

DETECTIVE DIXON: Yeah, Sure. You guys are smart.

DETECTIVE VALEZ: You think?

DETECTIVE DIXON: Absolutely. Face it: No matter how you look at it, kids are a hop in the ass. That never stops. By the time I hit Kindergarten I was a TERROR. The first thing I learned in school was to pull the fire alarm so we could watch the trucks come. I declared war on our next-door neighbor when he complained about our dog barking. I got a dead fish, put it on his carburetor and when his engine got hot it stunk up his Corvette forever.

DETECTIVE VALEZ: *(Reacts)* Eesh.

DETECTIVE DIXON: Oh yeah. The older I got, the worse I got. I'm telling you, I don't know why my folks never gave me back.

DETECTIVE VALEZ: 'Gave you back?'

DETECTIVE DIXON: Sure. They got me when I was four, so they knew what they had coming. You guys might have ended up adopting a little maniac like me.

(DETECTIVE VALEZ *realizes he undercut her decision*)

DETECTIVE VALEZ: You bastard.

DETECTIVE DIXON: And proud of it.

DETECTIVE VALEZ: Why didn't you tell me?

DETECTIVE DIXON: How could I know which way it would swing you?

(DETECTIVE DIXON's *phone*)

DETECTIVE DIXON: I'm vibrating. (*He squints at a text*) Who can read these little letters? Looks like a row of ants.

(DETECTIVE VALEZ *puts out her hand—he gives her the phone. She reads it.*)

DETECTIVE VALEZ: Susan Merrit's here. They're sending her up.

DETECTIVE DIXON: Let's do it.

DETECTIVE VALEZ: A petting zoo?

DETECTIVE DIXON: Llamas have a hell of a bite.

Scene 10

(*Police station—continued—the present, Interview Room One*)

(*Lights up on* SUSAN)

DETECTIVE VALEZ: Mrs Merrit. Thanks for coming down.

SUSAN: Of course.

DETECTIVE DIXON: We thought you'd want to hear it right away. (*To* DETECTIVE VALEZ) You want to tell her?

DETECTIVE VALEZ: Judge Guernsey agreed to a plea bargain for Samantha Sutton. Involuntary manslaughter.

SUSAN: Really? That's wonderful.

DETECTIVE VALEZ: Sentencing's next month, the sixteenth.

SUSAN: So it's over. It's finally over.

DETECTIVE DIXON: Seems that way.

SUSAN: Thank you. I know I haven't been easy to work with. I had a lot of anger, and you felt it.

DETECTIVE DIXON: How's your better half.

SUSAN: We haven't spoken. He's probably off on a dig.

DETECTIVE VALEZ: We wanted to give you all your confiscated clothing.

DETECTIVE DIXON: Jeez! I forgot! Her shoes aren't back yet.

DETECTIVE VALEZ: But you said—

DETECTIVE DIXON: Hey, I'm sorry. I wanted the lab to take another look at them.

DETECTIVE VALEZ: Why?

SUSAN: Exactly. Why? You just said Becca's girlfriend pled guilty.

DETECTIVE VALEZ: She did.

DETECTIVE DIXON: Right. *(To* SUSAN*)* but there's one thing you said that stuck in my craw. The "little rivers of blood".

SUSAN: I have no idea what you're talking about.

DETECTIVE DIXON: When you got to Becca's you say you called her name a few times, then tried the door. You pushed it open, you squeezed through, and that's when you saw her body. And her blood.

SUSAN: Yes. Right.

DETECTIVE VALEZ: But it didn't happen that way.

Scene 10B

(BECCA's apartment—before the murder)

(Lights up on BECCA's apartment, sound of knocks.)

(From the kitchen, first an arm can be seen, then, slowly BECCA crawls into view, moving toward the phone on the table by the couch)

SUSAN: (O S) Becca?

(BECCA reaches toward the phone but can't quite reach it as SUSAN enters with a handbag, holding the keys. She sees BECCA.)

SUSAN: Becca! Oh my God. (She crouches down by BECCA) Don't move. I'm going to get help.

BECCA: (Tries to speak, garbled) …She…

SUSAN: Be still. You'll be alright.

BECCA: Susan…

SUSAN: I'm right here. (Takes phone from the table)

BECCA: I'm so sorry…

SUSAN: "Sorry"? Why would you be…(For the first-time she sees the meleki on the floor. She stops dialing, leaves the phone on the rug, stands and crosses to pick up the meleki.) Is this…did Martin give you this?

BECCA: (Talking through her tears) It's my fault.

SUSAN: What is? What's your fault? I don't understand.

BECCA: The baby. I got an abortion.

SUSAN: You what?

BECCA: I had to.

SUSAN: Abort my baby?

BECCA: It wasn't yours.

SUSAN: WHO'S WAS IT?

BECCA: I didn't know... *(Gasps in pain)*

SUSAN: *(Putting it together)* It was yours and his.

BECCA: It wasn't. Please...help me!

SUSAN: No.

(BECCA reaches out for the phone on the floor before her, SUSAN kicks it away from her, toward the door. BECCA crawls toward it. SUSAN is still holding the meleki)

SUSAN: He never even told me he had this. But he told you. He gave it to you. He must think you're special. So special you should have his baby.

BECCA: No.

(BECCA crawls toward the phone, SUSAN kicks it again, it stops at the door. BECCA slowly crawls after it.)

SUSAN: This rock didn't hurt you enough. Not nearly enough.

(BECCA stops, still now. A moment passes. Another)

SUSAN: Becca?

(No response. SUSAN puts the meleki it in her bag. She picks up the phone, looks to BECCA, then looks at the phone, deciding.)

(Lights slowly fade.)

(In darkness, we hear the 9-1-1 OPERATOR)

OPERATOR: What is your emergency?

Scene 10C

(Police station—cont—the present-Interview Room One)

DETECTIVE DIXON: If you really pushed the door open to get in, you wouldn't have seen blood 'till you stepped in it. But when you were leaving, you would have stepped over it. Instinct. Your shoes were spotless.

DETECTIVE VALEZ: You took the murder weapon with you.

DETECTIVE DIXON: Pictures from the scene showed her phone on the table.

SUSAN: That's where it was!

DETECTIVE VALEZ: After you called 911, sure. But if it was there all the time, why would Becca crawl past it?

SUSAN: She might have been trying to escape!

DETECTIVE VALEZ: You. Meaning she was still alive when you got there.

DETECTIVE DIXON: Tell me this: How long did you have to wait for her to bleed out?

SUSAN: What's wrong with you? The woman who killed Becca confessed!

DETECTIVE DIXON: Martin didn't get Becca pregnant, Mrs Merit. Sam Sutton used your husband's sperm to fertilize her own egg, which Becca carried. He didn't know. Neither did Becca. You let an innocent girl die.

SUSAN: No! I didn't. You're wrong! I want my lawyer.

DETECTIVE VALEZ: We're not arresting you. We spoke to the Prosecutor's office. We can't prove it.

DETECTIVE DIXON: Yet.

DETECTIVE VALEZ: But, for now, you know you could have saved her life.

SUSAN: So what…what should I do?

DETECTIVE DIXON: Go home. Live with it.

Scene 10D

(Somewhere past time)

(Lights up on BECCA*)*

BECCA: You have it now, Mary told me your answer. But, no! It's not enough! All this pain and fear and heartbreak. All of us afraid, making choice after choice, not knowing if they're right or wrong. All of us in darkness, together, alone.

*(*BECCA *realizes. A piece of tile appears behind her.)*

BECCA: Like tesserae. Tiny pieces of broken tile. No one knows why they were made or where they should be. All they can see are those few tile fragments surrounding them. They can't know the design, the vision, or even if there is one.

(More pieces of tesserae can be seen emerging behind BECCA*.)*

BECCA: No simple blacks and whites, but so many slivers of color. What they create, together is beyond our view. We are embers, glowing in the dark. We are sparks, reaching for the light.

(A flash of the incomplete Madonna Of The Galilee mosaic bursts onto the screen before her.)

(Blackout)

END OF PLAY